DEFINING MOMENTS IN CANADIAN HISTORY

THE
FAMOUS FIVE

Weigl

Published by Weigl Educational Publishers Limited
6325 10th Street S.E.
Calgary, AB T2H 2Z9
Website: www.weigl.com

Library and Archives Canada Cataloguing-in-Publication Data available upon request.
Fax (403) 233-7769 for the attention of the Publishing Records department.

ISBN 978-1-77071-616-2

Printed in the United States of America in North Mankato, Minnesota
1 2 3 4 5 6 7 8 9 0 14 13 12 11 10

072010
WEP230610

Project Coordinator: Heather C. Hudak
Author: Penny Dowdy
Editor: Bill Becker

We gratefully acknowledge the financial support of the Government of Canada through
the Canada Book Fund for our publishing activities.

Contents

Overview

Women born in Canada before 1929 were defined by the law as non-persons. This meant that women did not have the same rights as men. Women could not run for office, be present in some courts of law, vote, and even own land if they were married. A number of women fought to have the laws changed, but the basic law, that women were not persons in the same way as men, remained.

Five women who had worked for women's rights in other areas decided to take the law to the Supreme Court of Canada. The judges agreed that women were not persons. At the time, Canada was still under British Rule in some areas of the law. The Canadian prime minister and the five women, known as the "Famous Five," asked that the Judicial Committee of the British Privy Council review the Supreme Court's decision. The Judicial Committee declared the Supreme Court's decision was wrong. Women were persons in the same legal sense as men.

Background Information

Emily Murphy - Emily Murphy was the first female judge in the entire **British Empire**. Her involvement in politics led to the Canadian government recognizing women as persons equal to men.

Irene Parlby - Irene Parlby was president of Alberta's United Farm Women and was the first **cabinet** minister in Alberta.

Louise McKinney - Louise McKinney was the first woman elected to the Legislative Assembly of Alberta and the first woman elected to a legislature in Canada, as well as the entire British Empire.

Nellie McClung - Nellie McClung worked diligently for women's and children's rights in Canada and served in the Legislative Assembly of Alberta.

Henrietta Muir Edwards - Henrietta Muir Edwards helped establish the National Council of Women of Canada and worked for women's right to vote.

IN THE 1800s, SINGLE WOMEN WERE ONLY ALLOWED TO SERVE IN A FEW JOBS, SUCH AS TEACHING OR WORKING IN OTHER PEOPLE'S HOMES.

MISS WILSON, CAN I BE A DOCTOR WHEN I AM AN ADULT?

NO, MARIE, ONLY BOYS CAN GROW UP TO BE DOCTORS.

IN MANY WAYS, WOMEN WERE MORE LIKE PROPERTY THAN PEOPLE. PARENTS OWNED DAUGHTERS UNTIL THEY MARRIED, AND HUSBANDS OWNED THEIR WIVES.

I TAKE YOU, JANICE, TO BE MY LAWFULLY WEDDED WIFE.

MARRIED WOMEN WORKED IN THEIR HOME, BUT THEY COULD NOT WORK AWAY FROM HOME TO EARN MONEY FOR THEMSELVES.

SOME CANADIANS MOVED TO THE WEST IN ORDER TO OWN FARMS AND RANCHES. THESE **HOMESTEADERS** DID NOT HAVE THE POLITICAL POWER THAT THE PEOPLE IN CITIES DID, AS THE POPULATION WAS NOT AS HIGH.

IF I WAS A HIRED MAN, I WOULD GET MONEY FOR MY WORK. SINCE I'M THE WIFE, I HAVE TO HELP FOR FREE!

AT TIMES, WHEN THERE WERE NOT ENOUGH MEN TO HIRE FOR LABOUR, WOMEN TOOK ON MEN'S JOBS. WOMEN OFTEN WORKED AS HARD AS MEN BUT DID NOT RECEIVE THE SAME BENEFITS FOR THEIR WORK.

FARMERS AND RANCHERS BECAME FRUSTRATED AT THEIR LACK OF POWER IN GOVERNMENT. THEY FORMED GROUPS TO SUPPORT THEIR CAUSES.

THE UNITED FARMERS OF ALBERTA WILL LET THE PEOPLE IN OTTAWA KNOW WHAT THE FARMERS NEED DONE.

UNITED FARMERS OF ALBERTA

THE FARMERS AND LANDOWNERS REALIZED THEY WOULD HAVE MORE POWER IF WIDOWS COULD OWN THEIR HOMES. IF WOMEN WERE ALLOWED TO VOTE, WESTERN CANADA WOULD HAVE MORE VOTES. GROUPS LIKE THE UFA BEGAN CALLING FOR WOMEN'S **SUFFRAGE**.

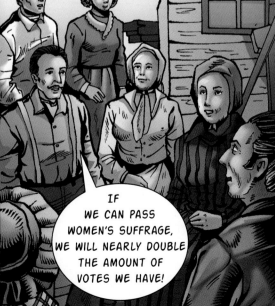

IF WE CAN PASS WOMEN'S SUFFRAGE, WE WILL NEARLY DOUBLE THE AMOUNT OF VOTES WE HAVE!

IMAGINE...I COULD VOTE FOR THE SCHOOL BOARD OR EVEN LEGISLATURE!

HENRIETTA MUIR EDWARDS SPENT DECADES FIGHTING FOR THE RIGHTS OF WOMEN. SHE HELPED ESTABLISH THE NATIONAL COUNCIL OF WOMEN OF CANADA (NCWC) IN 1893. THE GROUP WORKED TO IMPROVE THE LIVES OF WOMEN.

ONE OF THE FIRST THINGS WE NEED TO DO IS IMPROVE THE CONDITIONS OF WOMEN'S PRISONS.

EDWARDS MOVED TO ALBERTA WITH HER HUSBAND IN 1903. THERE, SHE ORGANIZED LOCAL GROUPS OF THE NCWC.

WHY SHOULD I JOIN THIS WOMEN'S GROUP?

WE NEED TO TEACH GIRLS AND YOUNG MOTHERS HOW TO CARE FOR THEMSELVES. WE DON'T HAVE HOSPITALS NEARBY LIKE WE DID BACK EAST, SO WE SHOULD DO A BETTER JOB OF TEACHING GIRLS HOW TO CARE FOR THEMSELVES. OUR SCHOOLS AREN'T DOING THAT NOW.

THOUGH SHE WAS NOT A LAWYER, EDWARDS SPENT MUCH TIME RESEARCHING LAWS RELATED TO WOMEN AND CHILDREN. SHE BECAME SUCH AN EXPERT THAT THE GOVERNMENT ASKED HER TO WRITE SUMMARIES AND HANDBOOKS OF THE LAWS.

HOW INTERESTING THAT WITH ALL THE LAWYERS IN OTTAWA, THEY NEED A WOMAN WITHOUT A LAW DEGREE TO EXPLAIN THEIR OWN POLICIES!

EDWARDS NEVER RAN FOR ELECTED OFFICE, BUT SHE WAS A GREAT SPEAKER. SHE FOUGHT FOR THE RIGHTS OF CANADIAN WOMEN AND CHILDREN.

THE **DOWER ACT** WOULD REQUIRE THAT A HUSBAND GET HIS WIFE'S AGREEMENT BEFORE SELLING THEIR HOME.

THE DOWER ACT PASSES! THANK YOU, MRS. EDWARDS, FOR WORKING SO HARD FOR THE BENEFIT OF CANADA'S WOMEN AND CHILDREN.

PARLBY WAS NAMED TO ALBERTA'S CABINET AS PART OF THE UNITED FARMERS OF ALBERTA. SHE WAS THE SECOND FEMALE CABINET MEMBER IN THE BRITISH EMPIRE.

CONGRATULATIONS, MRS. PARLBY. YOU ARE MAKING HISTORY!

I SWEAR TO UPHOLD MY DUTIES AS A CABINET MEMBER IN THE PROVINCE OF ALBERTA.

PARLBY FOCUSSED ON IMPROVING HEALTH CARE AND EDUCATION FOR WOMEN AND CHILDREN IN ALBERTA.

NOW WE WON'T HAVE TO TRAVEL FOR TWO DAYS TO SEE A DOCTOR.

LOUISE MCKINNEY WAS A LEADER IN THE **TEMPERANCE** MOVEMENT. SHE BELIEVED THAT ALCOHOL AND TOBACCO HARMED PEOPLE WHO USED THEM.

WE NEED TO SHUT THIS SALOON DOWN! THERE IS NO BENEFIT TO HAVING ALCOHOL IN OUR TOWN.

MCKINNEY ALSO THOUGHT LIQUOR AND TOBACCO COMPANIES HAD TOO MUCH INFLUENCE ON **POLITICAL PARTIES** IN CANADA. SHE RAN FOR OFFICE, BUT AS AN **INDEPENDENT** CANDIDATE. SHE WAS THE FIRST WOMAN ELECTED TO LEGISLATURE IN THE BRITISH EMPIRE.

WHEN I AM ELECTED, I WILL WORK TO HAVE THE ALCOHOL AND TOBACCO COMPANIES PUT OUT OF BUSINESS!

14

BEFORE MCKINNEY WAS ELECTED TO LEGISLATURE, A HUSBAND COULD SELL HIS HOME WITHOUT TELLING HIS WIFE. THE HUSBAND COULD TAKE THE MONEY AND LEAVE. THE WIFE AND CHILDREN WOULD BE HOMELESS, WITH NO SAY IN THE MATTER.

DON'T SAY A WORD TO MY WIFE UNTIL I'M OUT OF TOWN. THEN, SHE CAN TAKE THE KIDS AND GO LIVE WITH HER SISTER.

MCKINNEY WAS KNOWN AS A GREAT DEBATER. SHE PROTECTED THE RIGHTS OF DISABLED PEOPLE.

HOSPITALS FOR THE DISABLED ARE DEPLORABLE. WE CAN PASS LEGISLATION THAT ENSURES THESE PEOPLE ARE TREATED WITH DIGNITY.

WITH THE AID OF HENRIETTA MUIR EDWARDS, MCKINNEY HELPED WRITE THE DOWER ACT. THE LAW PREVENTED A HUSBAND FROM SELLING THE FAMILY HOMESTEAD WITHOUT HIS WIFE'S PERMISSION.

IT HAS BEEN AN HONOUR TO WORK WITH YOU, HENRIETTA.

I'M JUST PLEASED THAT WE WERE FINALLY ABLE TO GET THE DOWER ACT PASSED!

15

GENERALLY, ONLY MEN OF EUROPEAN ANCESTRY WHO OWNED LAND WERE ALLOWED TO VOTE. MINORITIES AND WOMEN WERE NOT.

POLLING PLACE

WHEN IS IT YOUR TURN TO VOTE, MOMMY?

I WON'T HAVE A TURN, DEAR. WOMEN ARE NOT ALLOWED TO VOTE.

SLOWLY, THROUGH THE LATE 1800s AND EARLY 1900s, WOMEN GAINED THE RIGHT TO VOTE IN LOCAL ELECTIONS IN SOME PROVINCES.

VOTES FOR WOMEN

WE WILL KEEP WORKING UNTIL WOMEN ACROSS CANADA HAVE THE RIGHTS WE DO HERE IN MANITOBA.

IN 1917, THE WARTIME ELECTIONS ACT MADE IT POSSIBLE FOR WIVES TO VOTE IN PLACE OF THEIR HUSBANDS IF THE MEN WERE SERVING OVERSEAS IN THE MILITARY. IF WOMEN WERE IN THE ARMED FORCES, THEY WERE ALSO ALLOWED TO VOTE.

The Tribune

Women Win Federal Franchise!

The "Famous Five" will become the first Canadian women to be honoured with a statue on Parliament Hill. They are the five Alberta women who, 70 years ago, fought Canadian lawmakers all the way to the Privy Council in Britain in their determination to have women recognized as persons and, therefore, able to serve as senators. The "Famous Five" are Emily Murphy, Nellie McClung, Henrietta Muir Edwards, Louise McKinney a...

The bronze sculptures will be a little larger than life size. The design of the five sitting figures suggests...

...able statue of th... ...eside that of Q... ...Centre Block,... ...Hill have been... ...Confederation... ...ceased prime...

IN 1918, THE FEDERAL GOVERNMENT ALLOWED WOMEN OF EUROPEAN ANCESTRY OVER THE AGE OF 21 THE RIGHT TO VOTE IN FEDERAL ELECTIONS. HOWEVER, SOME PROVINCES HAD NOT YET GIVEN WOMEN THE **FRANCHISE** IN PROVINCIAL ELECTIONS.

NELLIE MCCLUNG WORKED TO WIN WOMEN THE RIGHT TO VOTE. SHE WAS A WRITER AND TEACHER, AS WELL AS A WIFE AND MOTHER OF FIVE CHILDREN.

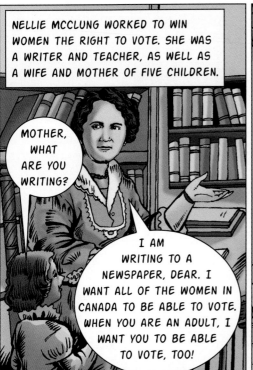

MOTHER, WHAT ARE YOU WRITING?

I AM WRITING TO A NEWSPAPER, DEAR. I WANT ALL OF THE WOMEN IN CANADA TO BE ABLE TO VOTE. WHEN YOU ARE AN ADULT, I WANT YOU TO BE ABLE TO VOTE, TOO!

MCCLUNG TRIED TO BRING ATTENTION TO THE CONDITIONS IN WHICH WOMEN LIVED AND WORKED. SHE SPOKE TO GOVERNMENT OFFICIALS, INCLUDING MANITOBA PREMIER RODMOND ROBLIN.

PREMIER ROBLIN, WOMEN NEED THE RIGHT TO VOTE. WE WOULD BE ABLE TO HELP MAKE LAWS THAT PROTECT WOMEN WORKING IN CONDITIONS LIKE THIS.

I DON'T BELIEVE THAT NICE WOMEN ARE INTERESTED IN VOTING. THEY ARE HOME WITH THEIR FAMILIES, RAISING THEIR CHILDREN. WHY DON'T YOU LEAVE PROBLEMS LIKE THE CONDITIONS OF THIS FACTORY TO THE MEN TO HANDLE?

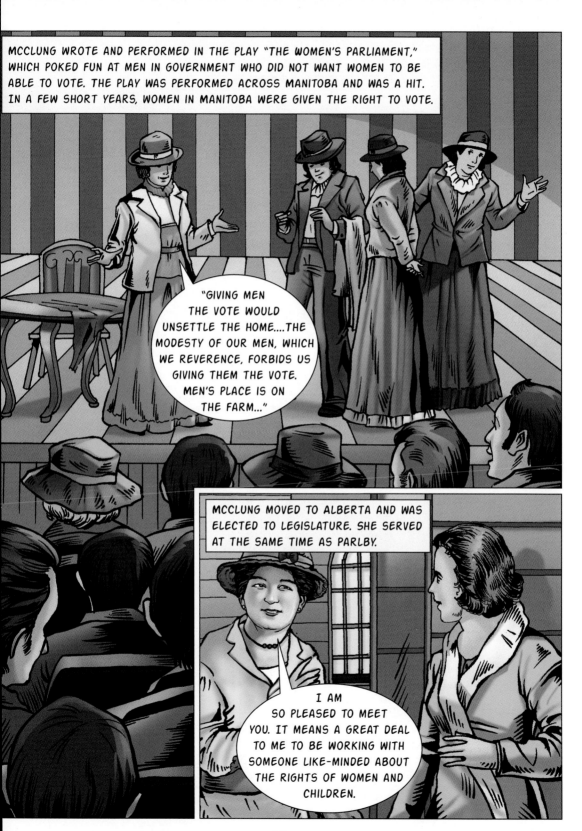

MCCLUNG WROTE AND PERFORMED IN THE PLAY "THE WOMEN'S PARLIAMENT," WHICH POKED FUN AT MEN IN GOVERNMENT WHO DID NOT WANT WOMEN TO BE ABLE TO VOTE. THE PLAY WAS PERFORMED ACROSS MANITOBA AND WAS A HIT. IN A FEW SHORT YEARS, WOMEN IN MANITOBA WERE GIVEN THE RIGHT TO VOTE.

"GIVING MEN THE VOTE WOULD UNSETTLE THE HOME....THE MODESTY OF OUR MEN, WHICH WE REVERENCE, FORBIDS US GIVING THEM THE VOTE. MEN'S PLACE IS ON THE FARM..."

MCCLUNG MOVED TO ALBERTA AND WAS ELECTED TO LEGISLATURE. SHE SERVED AT THE SAME TIME AS PARLBY.

I AM SO PLEASED TO MEET YOU. IT MEANS A GREAT DEAL TO ME TO BE WORKING WITH SOMEONE LIKE-MINDED ABOUT THE RIGHTS OF WOMEN AND CHILDREN.

EMILY MURPHY WAS A WIFE AND MOTHER IN ALBERTA. SHE PRESSURED LAWMAKERS TO GET THE DOWER ACT PASSED. UNDER THE ACT, WOMEN WOULD GET ONE-THIRD OF THE ESTATE IF THEIR HUSBANDS DIED.

REST ASSURED, YOU OWN THIS PROPERTY. EVEN THOUGH YOUR HUSBAND DIED, YOU WILL BE ABLE TO KEEP THE FARM, AND YOUR CHILDREN WILL HAVE A HOME.

WOMEN WERE NOT ALLOWED IN THE COURTROOM WHEN CASES WERE NOT APPROPRIATE FOR THEIR "DELICATE" EARS. THIS WAS **ARBITRARILY** DECIDED BY JUDGES AS CASES CAME TO COURT.

I'LL HAVE TO ASK YOU LADIES TO LEAVE. THIS WITNESS HAS **TESTIMONY** THAT PROPER WOMEN SHOULD NOT HEAR.

YOUR HONOUR, I DO NOT UNDERSTAND WHY WE SHOULD LEAVE. SHE IS TESTIFYING ABOUT HOW SHE BROKE INTO MY HOME. THIS IS MY BUSINESS!

MA'AM, MY ORDER STANDS. ALL WOMEN MUST LEAVE THE COURTROOM.

20

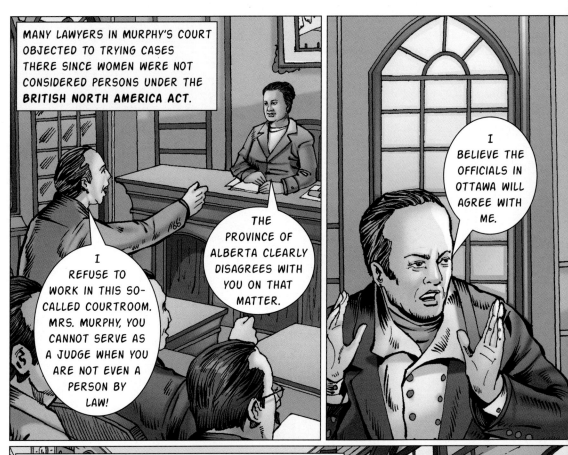

MANY LAWYERS IN MURPHY'S COURT OBJECTED TO TRYING CASES THERE SINCE WOMEN WERE NOT CONSIDERED PERSONS UNDER THE **BRITISH NORTH AMERICA ACT.**

I REFUSE TO WORK IN THIS SO-CALLED COURTROOM. MRS. MURPHY, YOU CANNOT SERVE AS A JUDGE WHEN YOU ARE NOT EVEN A PERSON BY LAW!

THE PROVINCE OF ALBERTA CLEARLY DISAGREES WITH YOU ON THAT MATTER.

I BELIEVE THE OFFICIALS IN OTTAWA WILL AGREE WITH ME.

THE BRITISH NORTH AMERICA ACT SAID THAT WOMEN WERE "PERSONS IN THE MATTER OF PAINS AND PENALTIES, BUT NOT IN THE MATTER OF RIGHTS AND PRIVILEGES."

YOU'RE A PERSON THAT CAN BE HURT OR BE SENT TO JAIL IF YOU COMMIT A CRIME...

...BUT I CAN'T SUE SOMEONE, VOTE, OR BUY PROPERTY ON MY OWN.

24

EVEN THOUGH THEY WON THE CASE, NONE OF THE FAMOUS FIVE WERE EVER NAMED TO THE SENATE.

"THIS DECISION MARKS THE **ABOLITION** OF SEX IN POLITICS. . . . PERSONALLY I DO NOT CARE WHETHER OR NOT WOMEN EVER SIT IN THE SENATE, BUT WE FOUGHT FOR THE PRIVILEGE FOR THEM TO DO SO. WE SOUGHT TO ESTABLISH THE PERSONAL INDIVIDUALITY OF WOMEN AND THIS DECISION IS THE ANNOUNCEMENT OF OUR VICTORY. IT HAS BEEN AN UP-HILL FIGHT."

WOMEN BEGAN SERVING IN THE SENATE STARTING IN 1930. PRIME MINISTER KING NAMED THE COUNTRY'S FIRST WOMAN SENATOR THAT YEAR, ONLY FOUR MONTHS AFTER THE RULING IN THE PERSONS CASE.

THE FLOOR RECOGNIZES SENATOR CAIRINE REAY MACKAY WILSON.

THANK YOU. I WOULD LIKE TO DISCUSS CANADA'S POLICY ON **IMMIGRATION**.

FOR YEARS, THERE WAS LITTLE RECOGNITION OF THE WORK OF THE FAMOUS FIVE.

THE CANADIAN GOVERNMENT HONOURS WOMEN WHO HAVE CONTRIBUTED TO UPLIFTMENT OF THE WEAKER SECTION OF SOCIETY.

EMILY MURPHY   (1868-1933)
IRENE PARLBY   (1868-1965)
LOUISE MCKINNEY   (1868-1931)
NELLIE MCCLUNG   (1873-1951)
HENRIETTA MUIR EDWARDS (1849-1931)

FIVE WOMEN WHO HAD WORKED FOR WOMEN OTHER AREAS DECIDED TO TAKE THE LAW TO SUPREME COURT OF CANADA

THIS IS THE PLAQUE THE GOVERNMENT MADE TO HONOUR THE FAMOUS FIVE. NELLIE, YOU ARE A HERO TO ALL WOMEN IN CANADA. I APPRECIATE THE REST OF YOU WHO CAME TO HONOUR THE FAMOUS FIVE.

THANK YOU PRIME MINISTER MACKENZIE.

MANY PEOPLE DID LITTLE TO HONOUR THE EFFORTS OF THE FAMOUS FIVE. HOWEVER, MEMBERS OF THE FAMOUS 5 FOUNDATION HELPED CITIZENS REMEMBER THE EFFORTS OF THE CANADIANS WHO HELPED PROMOTE THE RIGHTS OF WOMEN AND CHILDREN. IN 2000, THEY PLACED A **MONUMENT** ON PARLIAMENT HILL IN OTTAWA.

THE FAMOUS 5 FOUNDATION IS HONOURED TO PRESENT THIS MONUMENT. THE EXAMPLE SET BY THESE FIVE WOMEN WILL LEAD US TO HELP CANADIAN WOMEN PARTICIPATE AS CITIZENS.

THE $50 BILL RELEASED IN 2001 HONOURED SUFFRAGISTS, INCLUDING THE FAMOUS FIVE.

TODAY, THE FAMOUS 5 FOUNDATION HELPS WOMEN FIND A PLACE IN LEADERSHIP AND PUBLIC SERVICE.

WE NEED VOLUNTEERS TO PRESENT INFORMATION IN ELEMENTARY SCHOOLS NEXT WEEK. WHO IS AVAILABLE TO HELP?

Brain Teasers

1. In the 1800s, what was life like for women in Canada?

2. Why did the western provinces lead the way in giving women the right to vote?

3. What was the Persons Law?

4. What did the Persons Law prevent Emily Murphy from doing?

5. How was the Persons Law overturned?

6. How did the Dower Act change property laws for women?

7. Who was the first woman to serve as a senator in Canada?

Answers

1. Only single women could work outside the home. They could only work as housekeepers or teachers. Once they were married, women could not work. They could not own property, vote, or hold office.

2. The population in the western provinces was lower than in the east. Giving women the vote would increase the influence of the western provinces in federal decisions.

3. According to the Persons Law, women were not persons equal to men. Women did not have the same rights and privileges.

4. She could not serve in the Senate.

5. The Judicial Committee of the Privy Council of England ruled that the law was wrong, and that women were persons equal in rights and privileges to men.

6. A husband could not sell a family's property without his wife's permission, and if the husband died, the wife was guaranteed to receive one-third of the estate.

7. Cairine Reay Mackay Wilson was the first woman to serve as a senator in Canada.

Further Information

How can I find out more about the Famous Five?

Most libraries have computers that connect to a database that contains information on books and articles about different subjects. You can input a key word and find material on the person, place, or thing you want to learn more about. The computer will provide you with a list of books in the library that contain information on the subject you searched for. Non-fiction books are arranged numerically, using their call number. Fiction books are organized alphabetically by the author's last name.

Books

James, Donna, and Emily F. Murphy. *Emily Murphy*. Markham, Ont.: Fitzhenry & Whiteside, 2001.

Sharpe, Robert J., and Patricia I. McMahon. *The Persons Case: the Origins and Legacy of the Fight for Legal Personhood*. Toronto: Published for the Osgoode Society for Canadian Legal History by University of Toronto, 2007.

Gray, Charlotte. *Nellie McClung*. Toronto: Penguin Canada, 2008.

Websites

www.abheritage.ca/famous5
Alberta Online Encyclopedia, presented by the Heritage Community Foundation

www.famous5.ca
Official website of the Famous 5 Foundation

Glossary

abolition: to eliminate or do away with

arbitrarily: without thought or fairness

British Empire: Great Britain and all of the territories under its control

British North America Act: the law that established the independence of Canada and contains the country's constitution

cabinet: a group of advisers to the head of a government

constitutions: the physical makeup of an individual

Dower Act: Canadian law that ensured a husband received his wife's permission before selling their home

franchise: the right to vote

frontier: the area outside the settled part of a country

homesteaders: people who received public land on which to live

immigration: to come into a foreign country to live

independent: separate; not having connections with another

inherited: received after a person's death

monument: a building, pillar, stone, or statue honouring a person or event

petition: a formal written request made to an authority

political parties: groups of people organized to influence or direct the policies of a government

rural: related to the countryside

senator: a member of a law-making group or council

suffrage: the right to vote

temperance: a ban on alcoholic drinks

testimony: a statement made by a witness under oath, especially in a court

Index

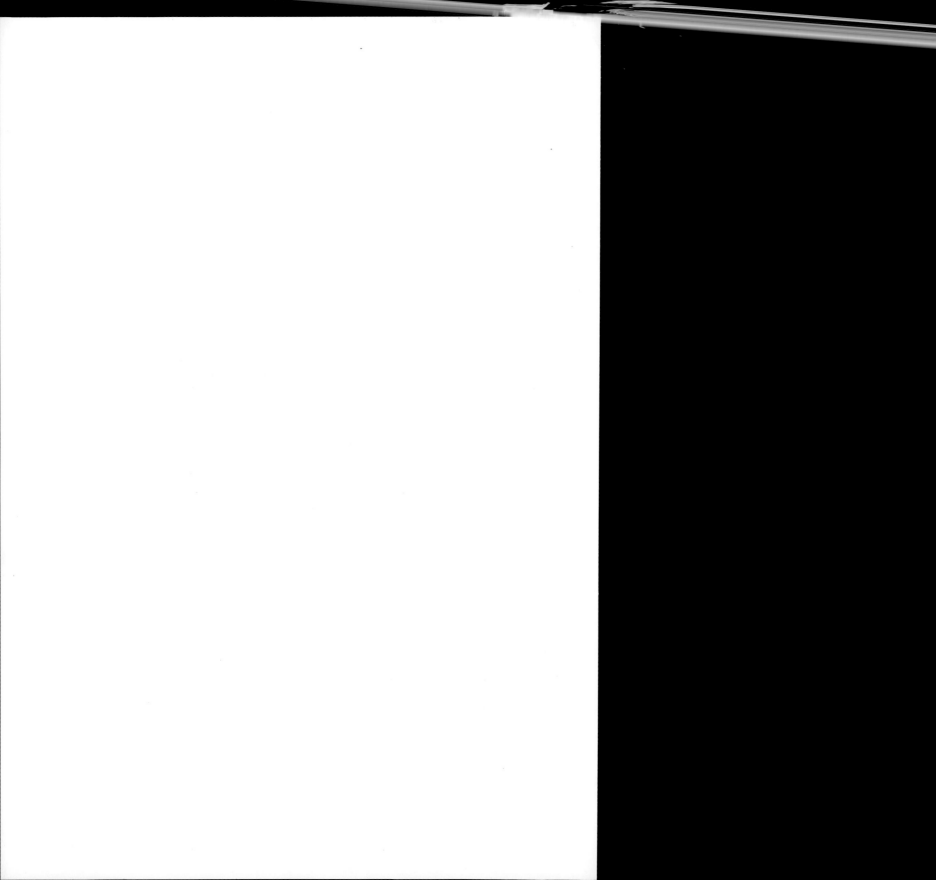